Thank you for showing interest in my Coloring book themed Michael Jackson.

If you liked my book please do leave a positive review that will help my book immensely. If you needed to suggest anything you want included in the book with your good review please do feel free to do so.

I have mentioned exactly what is in the book on the descriptions. So you may purchase my book if you are completely convinced about what you need.

For any further details about my cartoons and illustrations and to ask for any artistic assistance for your books, brands ot films it will be a pleasure to hear from you at remyfrancis@rembrandz.com

Printed in the United States of America

D1529513

Michael Jackson enjoyed martial arts, and was a black belt in karate.

Luna Society International named a crater on the Earth's Moon as "Michael Joseph Jackson" in honor of MJ, after his untimely death in 2009. Crater Michael Joseph Jackson is part of the Posidonius crater group, named for Posidonius of Apameia, a Greek Stoic philosopher, politician, astronomer, geographer, historian and teacher native to Apamea, Syria. Michael Joseph Jackson is the largest of the so-called "satellite craters" in the group, which numbers twelve in total, ranging in size from two to fifteen kilometers in diameter.

During the filming of a commercial, Jackson's hair and face caught fire, leaving him with second and third degree burns. Despite his horrifying experience Jackson did something incredible with his compensation money.

Shortly after the accident Jackson and Pepsi entered into compensation talks.

A short deliberation followed, before Pepsi compensated the singer with $1.5 million.

Despite this win, Jackson later went on to donate the money to the Brotman Medical Centre - one of the hospitals he was later treated in for his burns.

2023 © Remy Francis

Michael Jackson was supposed to attend a meeting at the World Trade Center on September 11, but he overslept and missed his flight.

Michael has set an unprecedented 39 Guinness world records.

2023 © Remy Francis

Jackson was twice nominated for the Nobel Peace Prize for his humanitarian work, first in 1998, and again in 2003.

2023 © Remy Francis

MJ TRIVIA

Jackson was one of the most charitable artists in the world who gave to the needy without any fanfare, most of the time, so although the exact amount maybe much more it is said that he has given over 500 million dollars in charity.

Michael Jackson went on to receive an honorary doctorate degree from Fisk University to recognize achievements of intellectual rigor comparable to an earned degree.

MJ was known for finishing at least one book every day because he read so voraciously. This truly reflected Michael Jackson IQ of 164 on how much he loved reading.

Michael tapes his fingers. Due to the distance from the stage, audience members couldn't always see his movements. By taping his fingers the white would catch the light so that people further back could see his hands.

The superstar made over 30 drawings of himself and other family members including his sisters LaToya and Janet Jackson.

During the Jackson 5 times the singer remembers that he really liked drawing when he was a child. When the Jackson boys were staying at Diana Ross' house, she encouraged them to develop their artistic skills.

The 10 Humanitarian Songs Of MJ

Cry (2001)

The Lost Children (2001)

Can You Feel It (1981)

Another Part Of Me (1988)

They Don't Really Care About Us (1996)

What More Can I Give (2003)

We Are The World (1985)

Man in the Mirror (1988)

In an interview, Michael Jackson told Soul Magazine an interesting fact about their first tour as Jackson 5. He said that in San Francisco and Los Angeles, it looked like the walls were falling, the way hundreds of fans came to the stage all together, that they have to practice getting away and be ready to drop everything and run. Like Jermaine dropped his guitar and took off at the Forum concert. In young MJ's words "we can always get a new guitar for him, but he'd be kinda hard to replace". Felt bad they usually can't finish the shows the way they rehearsed as always they have to run off stage, and they don't even get an opportunity to can't thank the audience.

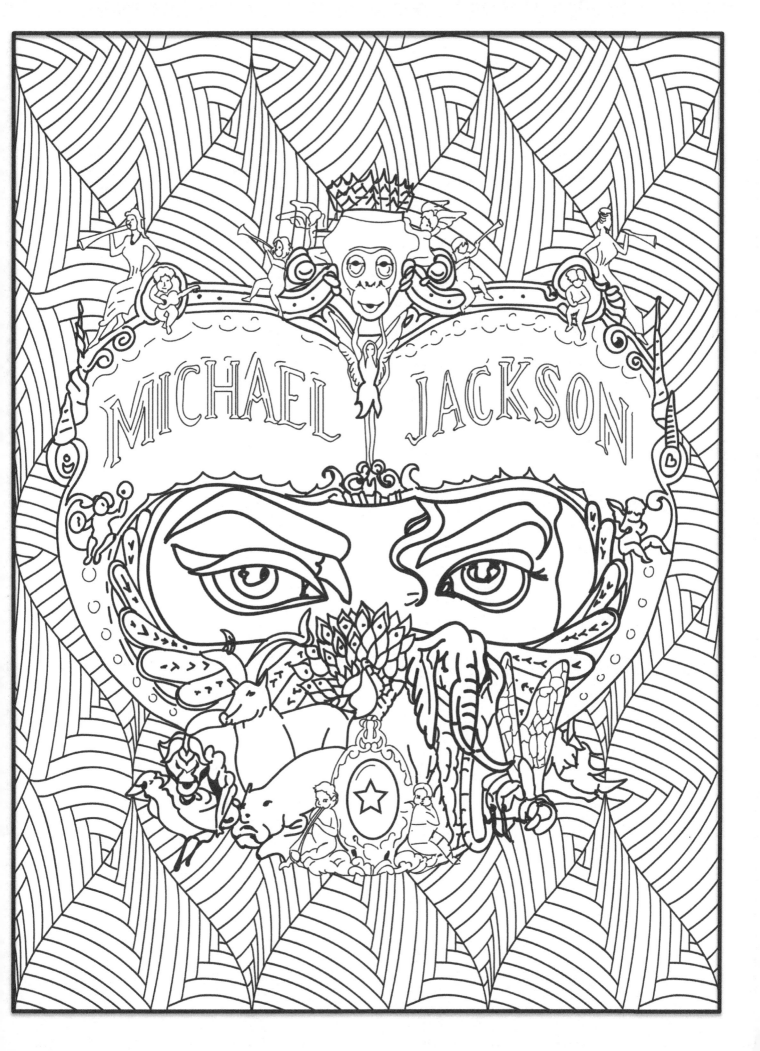

Made in the USA
Las Vegas, NV
25 November 2023

81417002R00050